Book of Harmony

The Symphony of Living

Copyright Notice

Dedication

This book is dedicated to all those in search of finding harmony in life – whether in thought, word, or deed.

- The Wisdom Buffet Writers

Preface

Harmonious Living? We all want it don't we? While the definition of harmonious is to be in agreement in feeling, attitude, or action, it is not always easy or realistic to see things in peaceful and fulfilling ways. But there are ways that you can sidestep the drama, work well together and find satisfaction in the give and take of daily life.   We have some great tips and insights to offer you that can make your life more content starting now!

In the third of an eight book series, *The Wisdom Buffet Writers* bring to you their latest book: *Book of Harmony, The Symphony of Living.* These eight contributing authors, all with the commonality of being Feng Shui Consultants, share with you their perception of what harmonious means to them and how we might capture it for ourselves.

We invite you to explore a collection of short stories, how-to-guidelines, and wisdom handed down from the masters; written in an easy-to-read format that can help you get started and keep you on the path to living your most harmonious life.

Table of Contents

Striking a Harmonious Chord

By Mia Staysko

Harmony is a basic principle of art and design. It is created when separate elements blend together in a pleasing way to create a cohesive whole. Though each aspect is unique, there is generally something that pulls them all together and makes them belong to each other. It is the same with all forms of design. A color, tone, shape or movement is repeated throughout the piece to create a sense of unity.

When I first met my husband Steve, he was a competitive performer, singing lead in a barbershop quartet, a form of a cappella singing, meaning without instrumental accompaniment.

A barbershop quartet is made up of four singers. The lead voice sets the pitch and the melody, while the baritone, base and tenor each sing the same song, but on a different note. In this style of music, all four individual voices work together to create a harmonious, singular sound: a four-point harmony. When it is done well, these four distinct voices blend together to create beautiful music.

All sound is vibration and each note resonates at a particular frequency. When all of the individual vibrations in a quartet are in harmony, the sound is pleasing to the ear. In addition to sound, this applies to all things in life; all things have a vibration and each vibrates at a particular frequency. Our thoughts and emotions are made up of vibrations. Our bodies and the physical world around us are vibrations. Sounds and words have a particular vibratory rate. So, if all things are, at their core, just vibrations, then the principles for creating harmonic music can be applied to creating a more harmonious life; one that is truly made of good vibrations.

Set the pitch

In a quartet, the first order of business is for the lead singer to set the pitch or the root note. All other notes are sung in harmony in relation to this note, so, if the lead is off pitch, the whole song sounds wrong.

No matter what aspect of our lives we are hoping to create beautiful music in, we must first determine what we hope to achieve. We must first set the pitch by setting our intention.

We start by asking ourselves "What guiding principles will lead us on our journey?" "What values do we hold dear?" "What do we want to achieve?" "What is our intention in doing this thing that we are embarking on?"

On a big-picture scale this might have

us looking at our overall values or at our long-term life goals. These might pertain to the way we want our families to function; our work life to unfold; or how to cultivate our relationships with ourselves and with others.

These same questions can be applied to smaller scaled aspects of our life as well. For instance, if we are working on a project at work, we can decide what will guide us. Will it be our company mission statement? Or will it be a desired outcome such as designing a better project or creating higher customer satisfaction?

If it is our intention to have a harmonious vacation with family, we might first need to determine what that looks like to us. Are we hoping for rest and relaxation or are we looking for an adventure? Unless the whole family has a relatively unified goal and a singular intention, it may be difficult to feel as though you've had a successful trip. If you've ever travelled with friends or family, you know that it can be challenging to keep everyone singing "Kumbaya."

Whatever aspect we are concerning ourselves with can be looked at through this lens of purpose and intent. Once we set the pitch, via our intentions, we have a base note for harmony. If something about a situation is feeling "off," we can ask ourselves what aspect is not harmonized with the intention.

We can check to see if all of the other components are in alignment with our root note. Each person, action and item added to the mix can be different, but they must speak to, and harmonize with, the overall intention. They must be a vibratory match, or at least within an octave or so.

Focus on your own note, while listening to all others

If you have ever tried to sing harmony, you

know that it is not easy to listen to the root note while simultaneously maintaining your own note.

This is also hard to do in life, for some of us, more than others. Rather than just focusing on what we are doing, living in harmony with our own goals and values, we feel the need to get the rest of the world to sing our same note. There are two big problems with this approach. The first is that, if we are all singing the same note, the song is boring and uninteresting. In order for us to create rich and well-rounded music together, we need both the top notes and the bottom notes. We need the rich base as much as we need the high tenor.

The second problem is that it is nearly impossible to get a bass voice to sing a tenor note. Therefore, we are not generally successful at getting other people to sing our note and we really should stop trying. We cannot control what other people do but we can certainly listen to others, carefully considering their particular take on things, while concentrating on holding our own perfect note. We can choose to change but we cannot choose to change others and trying to do this is a surefire way to create conflict and discord.

> *"All God's creatures have a place in the choir, some sing low, some sing higher…"*
>
> —Bill Staines

Instead of asking the world to change to come into alignment with our values and desires, we live more harmoniously when we simply live in alignment with them all by ourselves. If others see value in the way we live, perhaps they will be inspired to follow our lead, adding their own individual notes to our harmony. If not, that's fine. Diversity is what makes life interesting.

Pay attention to your own frequency

In a quartet, it is essential that each person

plays his or her part exactly as expected or the entire harmony is blown, creating discord. The word "discord," a harsh or unpleasant sound, essentially means we've missed the chord, that some piece of a 3 or 4 note chord is missing, or incorrect. If you've ever heard someone learn to play a guitar or other musical instrument, you know when a chord is hit and when it's been missed.

The principle of discord can be observed in life as well. When an emotion is out of alignment with how we wish to feel; when we speak out of alignment with how we wish to treat people; and when thoughts are incongruous with our intention to be kind, discord ensues. Usually, we can feel it. We create disharmony, which in turn creates discomfort, for others and ourselves. We may feel ill, things may begin to go wrong, or we simply feel uncomfortable about something. If you begin to feel this way, question it. See if you can determine where you've missed the chord. How are your thoughts, actions and words not in harmony with your higher aspirations? More importantly, how can you self-correct?

Our physical, mental, spiritual and emotional bodies all vibrate at a particular frequency at any given time. In some aspects of our lives, we may operate at high frequencies while in other life areas we may be vibrating at a much lower rate. It is said that love has the highest vibration, while fear is a low vibration emotion. When we are feeling like some aspect of our life is disharmonious, it can help to look at things from a frequency perspective.

For example, perhaps you have been working on raising your vibration around a certain topic. You've been meditating, contemplating, praying or using affirmations to increase your frequency. Suddenly, you find that you are often quarrelling with an old friend. It is likely that your friend is no longer in harmony with your current vibration and it may be time for you to let go and move on.

Pay attention to your own frequency and do your utmost to hold the note that you are meant to sing. You must know, and trust in, your place in the choir, so to speak. Each and every one of us has a part to play in this fascinating stew pot that we call life. We are all important, and no one more important than any other. This applies on both a macro and micro level. We are just as crucial to the overall planet's development as we are to the development of a project, to our family, and to our community. Work to increase your own vibration and higher vibration people and events will come in to your life to harmonize with that increased frequency.

Dissonance can be beautiful

If you've ever heard a barbershop quartet, you know that they are consummate entertainers, often using humor to entertain audiences. Doing something a little unexpected, like singing an off note on purpose, adds flavor and personality to the performance.

Sometimes you have to create a little chaos just to keep things interesting.

When life gets predictable and boring, or when you are stuck and unable to solve a problem it can help to do something unexpected. Try a different route to work. Go to a new restaurant. Switch desks with a colleague for the day. Put your yoga mat in a new spot!

Variety is the spice of life, and though we are more comfortable when our lives are harmonious, incongruity and dissonance can also have positive effects. They can shake us out of complacency and allow us to see life anew.

If things go off the rail, just go with it

Steve has a fabulous voice; unfortunately his memory is not quite as strong as his ability to hold a note. Because of this, when competing, he occasionally found himself on stage and suddenly lost, unable to remember the next line of the song they were performing. Since he was singing lead and the other three singers were harmonizing to his root note, they were forced to follow. There was no sense fighting it, everyone just followed along no matter where he was going, which was often in an infinite loop until he remembered the next line. Any other approach and the performance would be botched. The quartet embraced the unexpected and went with the flow, instead of against it.

We can work to chart our own course, to be masters of our own destiny, but let's face it; sometimes life can go off the rails. We can lose focus or an unexpected event may force us to change course. Being flexible helps us to weather storms. Stick to your core values, your base note, as it is your guide, but learn to improvise and to go with the flow, at least until you are back on track. Your life will be less stressful.

Ring a Chord

"The whole is greater than the sum of its parts."

—Aristotle

In a good barbershop quartet, the blending of four strong voices creates a pleasing whole. Unlike many other forms of vocal music in which one voice is prominent and other voices play only supporting roles, each voice in a quartet sings in a similar intensity. Though one member may play a more prominent role in one part of a song, another may step up later on. Overall though, each voice is as important as the next and without all four voices you simply would not have a quartet.

At times all four voices can sing with such intensity that the resonance of tones creates easily identified overtones or undertones. This occasionally creates the auditory illusion of a fifth voice and, in a barbershop quartet, this is called "ringing a chord." The combination of four perfect notes creates a fifth and the sum becomes greater than its parts.

This is the essence of harmony and when it is done perfectly, it is pure magic. When several things come together, all in alignment with a root intention, vibrating at similar frequencies, the music to our ears, our hearts, and our lives, is harmony.

Flow Like the Stream

By: Kim Klein

The more in harmony you are with the flow of your own existence, the more magical life becomes

—Adyashanti

One of my favorite bands in the late 1960s was Simon and Garfunkel. Not only did they write and sing songs that were a glorious mix of both raw realism and dreamy romanticism, but their timeless harmonies were pure and nothing short of absolute perfection. With different voices, styles, opinions and being two completely different personalities, they came together in the music that they produced and it all worked brilliantly.

Now, not always can our lives together produce such lovely melodies or poetic lyrics, but we can create a life of harmony once we acknowledge, respect, and accept each other's differences. When we put in the effort to understand and compromise, our lives can become magical, musical and harmonious.

It seems that to live in harmony should be a relatively easy feat because, truthfully, we all want to live a happy and peaceful life, don't we? I can see you nodding your head "yes" in agreement. As human beings with our many personalities, beliefs, thoughts and behaviors, getting along with others, including those we love, can be challenging and a constant balancing act of give and take.

About the same time that I was listening to Simon and Garfunkel on the radio, I stumbled upon the Japanese philosophy of Wabi Sabi. I was living in the Marshall Islands out in the Pacific in 1969 and became interested in all things Asian, from the foods that I ate to the philosophies of the many different cultures that surrounded me. As a young teen, it was the first time I became acutely aware that we all didn't need to be the same to live together; that life was a feast where every person brought something beautiful and authentic to the table.

Wabi Sabi is known as the "art of imperfection," or simply, finding beauty in all things; things that are imperfect, ever changing and impermanent. For example, when looking through Wabi Sabi eyes, we would find beauty in the odd shape of an heirloom tomato, character and distinction in the crow's feet around our eyes, the giving of a tree that has lost its leaves and the exquisiteness in our comfortable, but pilled and worn out sweater that has served us so well. These things have personality; we can see the life lived in them.

As people, places and things change with

time; we are reminded that we, too, along with everything else on the planet, are transient. When we accept this, we not only find that we appreciate every day of life that we are given, but we look at things quite differently. We can appreciate our aging bodies, faces, attitudes, and what we might consider our shortcomings. We've all posed that question to our self at one time or another, "If today was my last day on earth, how would I live my life?" And, no matter what we choose, whether spending time with our families, flying to Paris for lunch, or snuggling up on our sofa and watching our favorite movie again, they are all done with a new outlook and appreciation. Time does not stop for anyone. It is a limited resource. One we would be wise not to waste. And yet, until we are struck by some tragedy, illness or loss, we know this, we've heard it, but we forget to live it, and continue to sweat the small stuff. Without accepting change and accepting differences, we can never attain harmony. When we are trying to change someone, or something, there will, naturally, be resistance. As they say in Feng Shui, you cannot manipulate another's chi. This only leads to frustration and causes disharmony in our lives.

So, how do we achieve a state of living in harmony? We start at home, making peace with our self. We start with our own body, mind and soul. We get in alignment with who we are. And we do that by telling the truth. By being honest about who we are, what we want, and why we are here. All of our being has to be aligned. We can't have a mind that wants to be healthy, a body that only wants to stay in bed all day, and a soul that has no direction or feeling of purpose. There has to be alignment in order for us to effortlessly create the life that we want. When this occurs, there is a flow to our actions, thoughts and feelings;

a rhythm. As we live this way, we naturally convey that harmony to the world. When we have harmony in our own life, it will spill over and affect others.

Look at the stream: there are rocks in its way. Does it slam into them out of frustration? It simply flows over and around them and moves on! Be like the water and you will know what harmony is.

—Zen Story

When we live in the flow, we experience great amounts of joy, we treat others with love and respect, we honor our bodies and have a sense of purpose. There is a strong feeling of connection to the world around us. When we resist the flow, it is just the opposite. We repeat the same mistakes, joy in our life is lacking, we mistreat our bodies, soul and mind by eating poorly, not getting enough sleep, and by engaging in self-sabotaging behaviors.

We need to first get our own self in alignment and then we are more able to accept and honor others. We can only do this if we are willing to let go of old patterns and ideas about what we think should be and accept the way things are, in this very moment. In this way, we can feel a sense of peace and that all is right with the world. In this very moment.

It is also important to focus on what is working in our lives and to change the negatives into positives. For example, I remember when I would get so aggravated by slow drivers. From my driver's seat, I would fume while the people I was fuming at were oblivious to my anger and were probably enjoying the drive, listening to some beautiful classical music or having wonderful conversation. When I told my spiritual teacher this, she said, "Perhaps this is a message for you to slow down. Perhaps there was danger ahead and this caused you to miss out on some catastrophe. We will never know for sure but you must trust that you were exactly where you were supposed to be at the time, right behind that slow driving car." Well, whether this was true or not, I started to look at things a little differently after that. I slowed down. I learned to accept and appreciate that there might be a good reason for whatever was happening at the time.

It helps when we remember that most of us are much more alike than we are different. Most of us want the same things. To be loved, to love, to live in harmony and peace. Even in the case of a small spider. Now, that might sound ridiculous, but stay with me here. Even though a spider is usually no bigger than our fingernail, we are fearful of the spider because we don't understand him. He is scary, creepy and could bite us. When I

was young, I used to break down crying
if I even saw a spider, and would scream
for my dad to come and kill him for me.
It caused me great stress. So, we did a
little research together and learned that the
spider really had no intention of hurting
me, but naturally he would try to defend
himself from my deadly swats, brooms,
or Lysol cans. With that knowledge, it
relieved some of my fear and my world
didn't turn completely upside down at
the sight of a daddy long legs. I was able
to look at the spider with a sense of awe,
instead of fear, once I understood him a
little bit more.

The other important factor in being able
to live a harmonious life is to notice when
we are putting up resistance. When we feel
this happening, we should step back and
ask ourselves what is the true reason for our
resistance? It may be something that really
isn't that important or that big of a deal,

and it would be much easier for everyone if we just let it go. I'm sure you've heard it said, "Do you want to be right or do you want to be happy?" It is a matter of how important the battle is to you.

It helps to understand one of the main principles of Feng Shui, and that is that everything changes. We have no control over that. It is life. While we want things to stay the same: the kids to never grow up; the marriage to last forever; the body to never age; we don't have the control over these issues that we think we have. Suffering and pain come when we resist. Of course, there are many things in our lives that we can steer in the direction we want. That is free will and we should exercise it regularly. As we are reminded in the Serenity Prayer, "God grant me the serenity to accept the things I cannot change, the courage to change the things I can, and the wisdom to know the difference."

I find that when life gets complicated or frustrating, getting out in nature can help restore my sense of balance. We can learn a lot about harmony by observing nature. Have you ever watched a flock of geese fly overhead as they migrate south for the winter? They call out from above and we naturally look up as if answering them. But if you've ever really watched them, or studied them, they teach us all we need to know about living in harmony with one another.

I first fell in love with the Canadian Snow Goose when, as a young girl, I saw a movie starring Richard Harris called "The Snow Goose." It was an inspirational story about a disfigured, reclusive older man living in an abandoned lighthouse on the Essex's Great Marsh and a young orphan girl who were brought together by a snow goose that had been wounded by hunters. Their friendship blossomed while caring for the injured bird. It was a story that stayed with me through my entire life. It was haunting and sad, but beautiful, in that it conveyed the power of love and friendship.

Since that day, I have been keenly aware when geese are around me, or when I hear them broadcasting their presence as they go flying by. They fascinate me and I started to read all about them. I was amazed at the way they fly in their V-formation, with the lead goose like an orchestra conductor, keeping them all in tune. When the lead goose tires, he takes a break and retreats to the end of the line and another bird that is stronger will take his place. They support one another. They work together. If one of the birds gets sick or extremely tired, two other geese will fall out of formation and fly with him, to protect him, until he either dies or recovers. I doubt very much that when the lead goose declares he is tired that the others start forming negative opinions, such as, "What a loser," "He's a weakling," or "Geez, I hate a quitter." No, they know that everything changes and they adapt to those changes in the best way possible. When they pull together, it makes the journey much easier for all of them and they are able to reach their destination.

Humanity is one family, connected and interwoven. It stands to reason that life becomes much more joyful when we work together rather than work against each other. There is an old Native American saying that sums it up beautifully and one that we would be wise to adopt as our own: *No tree has branches so foolish as to fight among themselves.*

Emotional Balance

By Jim Thomas

We are what we think.
All that we are arises with our thoughts.
With our thoughts we make the world.

—Buddha

Dhammapada

Achieving harmony, balance, and inner peace are major themes in spiritual teachings; however, the spiritual community is often guilty of complicating the attainment of these desired qualities by discussing them in abstract, ambiguous, or mystical terms. There is plenty of information about positive thinking, mantras, crystals, aroma therapy, and chakras, and while all these practices have their merit, they often obscure the most basic truth from those of us seeking balance in our lives, that the most powerful thing we can do to balance our lives is to become aware of our emotions.

Everything in this universe, at its most fundamental level, is energy and emotions are no different. Emotions are the physical representation of thinking; they mirror the quality of our thoughts. The quality of the emotion you experience at any given moment is a direct reflection of the quality of thought that you are thinking at a conscious or unconscious level. If you are experiencing the emotions of anger, sadness, or jealousy, then you are having these exact same thoughts. Conversely, positive emotions indicate that your thoughts are of the same quality.

If we have awareness of our emotions then we have awareness to our thoughts, which is very important as our thoughts determine what we focus on, how we focus on it, and how we respond to situations. We can think of beliefs as thoughts that we have convinced ourselves to be true. If someone believes that they are unappreciated by another person, this person will focus on the ways that they are being unappreciated by the other person. Because this person's attention is on being unappreciated, they focus on anything that the other person does that supports this belief. For example, this person may have noticed that the other person has not wished them a happy birthday, leading them to believe that this is another piece of proof that they are unappreciated, when in fact, the other person may have completely forgotten as they had things on their mind. This belief then influences how they interact with the other person as well as with themselves. It is our beliefs that shape our lives and eventually our destiny as our destiny is forged by the beliefs we hold and the actions we take. This it is what Buddhism refers to as karma. Our karma is the thoughts, words, and actions that we engage in.

Our behaviors are determined by our thoughts and our emotions inform us of our thoughts. The problem is that we live in a society where emotions are not honored, which is why most of us avoid or deny our emotions. Most of us have been conditioned by our parents, our upbringing, or our society to not express our emotions or to get in touch with them. In doing so, we are ignoring the gift that emotions offer us: a window to our thoughts, including those thoughts that may have been suppressed from our own awareness; our lives are unbalanced because we have lost touch with ourselves. Instead of tuning into ourselves, we distract ourselves by focusing on what is happening outside ourselves. We pour our daily lives into working, shopping, texting, cell phones, computers, our relationships, watching television, eating, drinking, smoking, taking drugs, and focusing on our problems. Most, if not all, of our problems, be they emotional, physical, financial, interpersonal, or spiritual, are rooted in the fact that we have become strangers to our inner world, while getting caught up in the world outside of ourselves, which causes our lives to be unbalanced.

The Buddha wrote, *"You are the source of all purity and impurity. No one purifies another."* What is meant by this statement is that no one but yourself can bring purity or impurity into your life, this is because you are the source of all your experiences. Your authentic nature is consciousness and everything you experience in your life, including your sense of being a person, arises from consciousness. Think about it, you are reading this book because you want to bring balance into your life. How could you read a book or desire balance if you were not aware of it, just as how would you know that your life was unbalanced if it was not for awareness, which is focused consciousness.

The most powerful way to obtain balance in your life is to bring awareness to your emotions and thoughts. When we do this, we become aware that who we are is not our emotions and thoughts. The ego is created by our identifying with our thoughts, emotions, physical body, or anything else that we have awareness of. Balance and inner peace arise when we experience and know that we are the observer of thoughts and emotions, rather than identifying with them. When we identify with them, we become them. The Buddha also wrote, *"All that we are is the result of what we have thought. The mind is everything. What we think – we become."*

The following are some simple strategies that you can use to develop greater self-awareness. The first strategy is to listen to your emotions and honor them. Your emotions are like a GPS system that will provide you with the signals that you need to align yourself with the rest of life or the universe. You are the physical manifestation of consciousness and that consciousness manifests itself in physical form, so you are in no way separate from consciousness or the universe itself. When you experience positive emotions, it is an indicator that you are aligned with the universe. When you experience negative emotions, the universe is sending you a message that you are out of alignment. The key then is to spend your time engaged in those things that result in you experiencing positive emotions. There are times when we need to do things that we do not enjoy, which is okay, if we perform them with a sense of acceptance. Our problems occur when we engaged in thoughts or behaviors despite the fact that we have a sense of resistance to them. If you need to do something that you do not want to do, be sure to develop an attitude of acceptance and release your resistance before proceeding. If the resistance persists, do not engage in the activity as you will be out of alignment. This simple exercise will help you restore your sense of balance and wellbeing.

The second strategy is breath meditation. Follow these steps:

1. Sit down in quiet place where you will not be distracted.

2. Make yourself comfortable and take a few deep breaths.

3. When you are feeling relaxed, close your eyes and breathe normally.

4. Place your awareness on your breath

and follow it as it enters your body during inhalation and leaves your body during exhalation.

5. Keep your attention on your breath. If your catch your mind wandering, gently return your attention to your breath.

During this exercise, do not judge anything, including yourself. Do not judge yourself if you have trouble keeping your concentration or for any thoughts that you may have. The most important thing is to be aware when your mind wanders and that you return your focus to your breath. By keeping your attention on your breath, you are strengthening your concentration, while catching yourself when your mind wanders strengthens your awareness to the activity of the mind. If you practice this consistently, you will reach a point where you will notice that your mind becomes less turbulent with thoughts. Perhaps more importantly, you will develop an awareness that there is a separation, or a distance, between you and your thoughts and emotions. Stated more specifically, you develop less self-identification with these things. When this occurs, you will automatically develop greater balance in your life as you will be less impacted by your thinking and your emotions, while having greater awareness of them.

An important principle in Buddhism is the oneness of life and its environment. In other words, you and your environment are inseparable. Your inner life will influence your environment as your environment will influence your life. The room of someone who is depressed will very likely reflect how that person feels inside. Conversely, a cluttered or untidy environment can affect how we feel. Earlier in this chapter, it was explained everything in this universe is made of energy. The ancient practice of feng shui is about influencing the flow of energy, known as chi. When the flow of energy is disrupted, disharmony occurs in our wellbeing and our daily activities, including our work, our interactions with others, and the level of our financial success. Feng shui works to bring back balance to our environment through the strategic placement of furniture and other objects within the home, work, or other living space. While feng shui is most often associated with the making changes in our living spaces, chi is found in the body, in nature, the Earth, and the cosmos.

The balancing of energy is rooted in the concept of Yin and Yang, which is the study of interdependency of opposites. This interdependency mirrors the Buddhist principle of dependent origin, which states that nothing in this universe can arise independently of anything else. Darkness cannot exist independently of lightness, war cannot exist independently of peace, and hate cannot exist independently of love. In dualistic perceptions, we fragment reality by seeing things as being separate, such as happiness is the opposite of sadness. From the perspective of Yin and Yang, happiness and sadness are the two sides of the same coin. Happiness can only exist if sadness exist, and sadness is only possible because happiness is possible.

A balance or imbalance of energy within us will have an effect on not only on ourselves but on our environment as well, based on the principle of the oneness of life and the environment. By being aware of our emotions, by focusing on the things that we have positive emotions for, or at least acceptance for, we will be able to balance our energy and align with the energy of the universe. Additionally, by being balanced, we are more likely to be sensitive to how we design our living space, which is one aspect of feng shui. Conversely, if our energy level is unbalanced, using feng shui to create a balanced living space will affect us in a positive manner, which leads to an important point about energy that is often misunderstood. We do not share energy with other people, meaning other people cannot sap your energy from you, though it may feel like it sometimes; rather, your energy level influences other people's energy level and vice versa. If I am not in touch with my emotions and hang around a negative person, that person is not draining my energy; rather, I am allowing myself to lower my energy level by placing my focus on their negativity. Conversely, if I have a low energy level and someone with a very high energy level walks into the room, they can cause me to raise my energy level.

This phenomenon is based on the law of attraction. Healers are those people who are very aware of their emotions and energy levels, allowing them to maintain a high energy level when they are around others who have lower energy levels.

We often hear about the importance of eating a balanced diet and living a balanced life style. At this point you may begin to wonder if all this is too much work, or if it is really worth it. The answer to this question is very easy, just look at the consequence of not living a life of balance; the evidence is everywhere you look. Obesity, disease, aggression, violence, depression, addictions, stress, problems sleeping, eating disorders, and the destruction of the environment are just a few examples of what happens when we do not live a balanced life, when our energy is imbalanced. The good news is that by just balancing your energy level, how you eat and how you live your life will automatically come into balance. You will find yourself desiring healthy foods, while losing interest in those foods that are not nourishing. As for your life style, you will find yourself engaging in activities that support you emotionally and physically. Even more powerfully, you will positively affect the lives of others.

The Way of a Harmonious Life

By Mary Jane Kasliner

"When we feel, a kind of lyric is sung in our heart. When we think, a kind of music is played in our mind. In harmony, both create a beautiful symphony of life."

—Toba Beta

Many of the great writers and philosophers have pondered a life lived in harmony. I would imagine living such a life would be likened to experiencing heaven on earth. But how do we go about doing that? Toba Beta gives us an idea in her quote: *"When we feel, a kind of lyric is sung in our heart. When we think, a kind of music is played in our mind. In harmony, both create a beautiful symphony of life."* Sounds so simple in theory, however the relationship we have with ourselves and what matters to us is usually in conflict with the relationship we have with the world around us. When this happens, we experience stress. Why? A little thing called resistance takes front and center and we refuse to give in and accept what is. When this occurs it is impossible to align our thoughts, actions, and relationships with our true values; the result is disharmony.

The Law of Least Effort

"Nature does not hurry, yet everything is accomplished."

—Lao Tzu

In Deepak Chopra's book, The Seven Spiritual Laws of Yoga, he discusses "The Law of Least Effort." This law states that nature's intelligence functions with effortless ease. Just looking at the natural ebb and flow of the ocean tides or blooming flowers supports this law. If you notice flowers and trees do not strain to bloom but rather there is grace, perfect timing, and finesse when it comes to transforming its energy. *The Law of*

Least Effort tells us that we can do less and accomplish more when we let go of resistance and simply accept what is.

There must be more to living a life of harmony than just learning how to accept 'what is.' And in fact, there is. If we continue from the standpoint of nature, there are in fact other components that fulfill the elements of harmony and balance; albeit these components do contain many paradoxes. For example, if you observe the great forces of nature, it is obvious that there is a level of detachment, yet compassion, between these interacting forces. For example, trees spread their roots deeply into the earth but are not attached to the earth. Trees recognize the nurturing qualities Mother Earth provides and display their compassion through an exchange of nutrients released for other living things to feed upon.

There are other paradoxes we see in

nature, too. If you observe a flower blooming there is a joyful expression in its petals — an enjoyment of life if, you will. However, flowers do not cling to this life. They accept their eventual decay as part of the process. They do not obsess over how perfect their color, shape, or texture is during their lifetime. They are simply indifferent to success or failure of their growth patterns.

Other paradoxes of harmony can also be seen through the eyes of the Taoist sage. Taoism is a philosophy of simplicity and noninterference. It is a Chinese philosophy that advocates a simple life allowing a noninterference with the natural course of things. The Taoist sage is a man of honor, and yet he does not reap honor. He lives a life of highest moral order but ignores ethics and morals. He achieves but does not strive. He knows the answers but prefers to remain silent. These are paradoxes, yet they define perfect harmony the same way nature itself seems to be a harmonious blend of such paradoxes.

Living Close to Nature

"Nature is the art of God."

—Ralph Waldo Emerson

Even in the midst of city chaos, not a day goes by that man's eyes won't fall upon some aspect of nature's beauty, natural rhythm, and flow of life. Whether it's the sunrise and sunset, tree branches as they fold in the wind, a bird's fluttering wings, or swollen clouds drifting along the gray sky, the earth's sights and sounds ignite the human spirit and induce a sense of harmony.

Remaining intimately close to the instinctual aspects of nature even amongst society's shifting struggle to reach some imaginary apogee makes all the difference when it comes to experiencing a life of harmony. But how can we do that without becoming lured into the artificial corporate environment of greed and envy? It is simple. Spend time in nature every day and seek its natural qualities in your own environment. Choosing natural design elements such as real wood, natural stones, metals, and fresh water features are perfect ways to bring the outdoors inside. There are countless benefits to surrounding yourself with nature's essence including ways to bring balance into your life. For example, trees teach us to be flexible in life. How? Their flexible branches allow it to withstand different weather conditions. In flexibility there is strength and resilience. If we maintain a flexible position in our attitude and viewpoint, then we naturally see eye-to-eye with others.

Trees also teach us acceptance through their ever-changing patterns of shedding leaves and sprouting new shoots. This is what keeps them alive and filled with vitality. If you accept change as part of the natural order of things, then your life will gain new vitality; you will have a zest for living and a feeling of being balanced.

Wind teaches us how to let go and be free in life. Wind does not resist but rather is free in spirit. When we let go of resistance life is joyful, harmonious, and abundantly blessed. Wind energy also teaches us to rely on our intuition — the voice of the higher self. When we listen to the seer within and use "the word" impeccably, then we experience heaven on earth.

The sky teaches us to be free-spirited. To let go completely means to let go of what others may think, to release conventional behavior, not to let anything bog you down. Father Sky implores you to march to the beat of your own drum by allowing your personality to become boundless, full of life, well-rounded, interesting and happy-go-lucky.

Mother Earth teaches us to be humble and truthful. The earth doesn't rank different aspects as being better than others; all parts are equal. When you realize that no one is superior to another and honor our differences, accomplishments can be shared with grace. Seeking truth is the cornerstone to harmony. The earth is always true to itself. It doesn't seek to destroy. If we are true to ourselves first, then it will be easy to be true to others and live in a state of balance.

The element of water in nature teaches us to persevere and look for assistance on our path. Trying to do it all only leads to frustration and imbalance. When we seek others out on our life's journey, then abundance follows, anxiety dissipates, and harmony takes hold.

The fire of the sun teaches us to see things clearly and rely on insight. You can become the creator of your own destiny and, in the process, empower yourself and others. Sun energy reminds us of the simple pleasures of summertime where everything comes out to play: flowers are in bloom, and laughter is in the air. Without the element of joy, life is stressful and out of balance.

The majestic mountains of the earth exude a sense of stillness. When we practice stillness through meditation we maintain composure and find a greater meaning in each experience and unleash potential power. Mountain energy also teaches us to value our efforts in life and not just the successes. This requires patience so we can discover who we are and who we are not, which leads us to the axis of our being where everything revolves and a cheerful acceptance of life can be found.

Communing with nature feels like coming home. It has a way of energizing the spirit, keeping us balanced and joyful.

One can feel the wind communicating, full of life and intelligence, while the sunlight, with all of its warmth and vitality, energizes everything in its path. There is an intertwining of energy that dances between us and Mother Nature where harmony exists.

Equanimity

"When there is no desire, all things are at peace."

—The Tao

The Taoist sage does not rely on external things to provide him with a harmonious spirit. When we are dependent on things like wealth, status, popularity or success we easily crumble in the face of defeat, failure or loss.

To live means to have balance in our thoughts and actions. Excess of any kind leads to imbalance and suffering; however, the fact is that nature does not allow us to move away from this balance. Everything in nature grows, stabilizes and withers away. Man, on the other hand, fights against this law not by living a balanced life but resorting to gimmicks that promise to break this cycle. This simply creates a vicious cycle with no end in sight.

For equanimity to arise, we must accept life experiences for what they are — the good, the bad and the ugly — while not reacting either negatively or positively. The only way to have a balanced life is to stay rooted in a state of calm acceptance no matter what the outcome. Although it can be difficult to remain calm when things are not going as planned, it is the way to harmony. Should we choose to fight against what is, the universe will respond with repeated circumstances that expose us to unpleasant situations. Unless we move forward and adjust our behavior to these disagreeable circumstances, the cycle will repeat and suffering will continue.

Simplicity

"Simplicity is the ultimate sophistication."

—Leonardo da Vinci

Living a modest life with little desire and almost no expectation can be difficult in a world dedicated to material gain and vanity. However, living a simple life has its perks. When you choose to live with enough, but not in excess, you tap into the essence of a good life. You eliminate all the "stuff" so your life becomes unfettered and there is more time to do what you *want* to do instead of what you *have* to do.

Choosing to live a simpler life makes it easier to balance your time between work, home and other responsibilities. When there are fewer distractions in your life, there are fewer things competing for your time. Taking that long walk, visiting with a friend, or curling up with your favorite book becomes a reality rather than a wishful thought.

'Less is more' is a precept for minimalist design. This phrase cuts to the chase when it comes to living simply. The less we put in our environments and in our minds, the better off we will be. Once we voluntarily decided to let go, we eliminate the worry and anxiety that come with trying to maintain everything. We reduce the busyness factor which of course is activity with no real purpose. We begin to recognize all those things we do that have no real purpose. Life is too short to waste it on being busy. Instead, choose to live simply and reacquaint yourself with the fundamental beauty of nature. You'll come to appreciate the natural elegance of Mother Nature and feel more balanced as a result.

Living Mindfully

"Each morning we are born again. What we do today is what matters most."

—Buddha

Mindful living is attending to the present moment without judgment. It involves nothing more than being in a state of awareness — noticing moment to moment what is happening and then releasing it until the next experience arises. Yoga follows this same mindful concept. One becomes a witness to the breath, making no judgments but simply allowing the next breath to occur.

When we take the role of being the witness in life rather than judge and jury, it has a calming effect on our brain. The more we practice this approach, the more our brain wants it. The "monkey mind," as Buddhists call it, slows down and a new peaceful way of being takes hold. This is the key to living a harmonious life — letting go of the mind chatter and being in the here and now. After all, life unfolds in the present.

When you become mindful you begin to realize you are not your thoughts.

Instead you awaken to the experience of the thoughts. When you tune into this behavior, stress is reduced, the urge to be impulsive or reactive wanes, and the immune system is activated in a positive way. So how can one begin to live more mindfully? Here are a few simple things you can do to get the energy moving in the right direction:

- Stop over-thinking things. Just let go and be in the moment.

- Let go of the past or wondering about the future and experience what is happening right now.

- Practice tuning into your breath. This simple act will automatically move you from an ego state of mind to feeling more connected to yourself and others.

- Move into a state of flow. Flow

occurs when you are so engrossed in a task that you lose the concept of time.

- Meet a challenge head-on instead of resisting it. Resistance will only magnify it.

- Take notice of new things in every situation. This will automatically shift you from 'Monkey Mind' into the present moment.

- Think of yourself as an eternal witness and just observe the moment.

Silence

"Hello darkness, my old friend,
I've come to talk with you again,
Because a vision softly creeping,
Left its seeds while I was sleeping,
And the vision that was planted in my brain
Still remains
Within the sound of silence."

—Simon and Garfunkel

The sound of silence — isn't that a contradiction? Is there really a vision of silence or, for that matter, emotions contained in silence? Simon and Garfunkel seem to think so, and I tend to agree with them. If you've ever experienced entering "The Gap" during meditation there is a definite softness that creeps in and a far-off humming sound as if you can hear the vibration of the universe. It is a feeling of profound peace.

A keynote to a harmonious life is to cultivate silence — certainly a challenge when we are constantly bombarded by noise, social media, and the need to be overly busy. Silence can be a spiritual experience. It can also be a treasure. Finding the quietude in between the sounds and activities of the day can act as a grounding mechanism that will deepen your connection to yourself and others.

Building more silence into your daily life

can be as simple as taking a quiet moment before bed or contemplating a peaceful image. The idea is to fall into the realm of nothingness so you can cultivate spaciousness and deepen the connection to your soul. The benefits of devoting a few short minutes a day to silence can reduce stress, improve mental clarity, expand insight, and enhance well-being.

Silence is accessible to each of us. It doesn't require a special password or cost anything. It is a simple choice that can uncover the intelligent voice within and lead to pure joy.

Music to Die For

By Katherine Graham

Twice in my adult life, just upon waking, I have heard the most amazing music. You could compare it to Beethoven with a galactic back-up band. It is said that in Heaven you hear the angels sing and that it is the most beautiful harmony conceivable. I have no proof that what I heard was angels or cosmic beings but, for a moment, it felt as though I was caught between worlds; lingering just long enough to be consciously aware of the most intensely glorious sounds I have ever heard.

I once imagined Heaven's music to be like Christmas mass when the chorus rings through the vast space of the Cathedral, resounding in the rafters with a timeless purity. I have been so moved by the music at mass that tears will, involuntarily and silently, run down my cheeks. I find this hard to describe because it moves me on a deep spiritual level.

The chorus at church is beautiful, wonderful, but falls flat compared to what I heard upon waking those two mornings. What I experienced sounded very much like Classical music resonating with an unquantifiable vast body of beings, undulating chord progressions and shifting base lines. What's more, while I was listening, I felt complete inner peace along with something else indescribable- like I was floating or being suspended by an effervescent string, sparkling and gently vibrating in the music.

I believe I heard what everyone will one day hear again when they return to where their souls first departed- call it dying, going to Heaven, reaching the other side or what's at the end of the tunnel. Mine is a gentle knowing, a comfortable familiarity, like being back in the living room of the house you grew up in and all the same furniture is still in exactly the same places. When I awoke, I knew that I knew this place and that I had never really departed; it existed just on the other side, veiled and hidden, but there all the same.

I attempted to tell my husband about it once and as the words were coming out, I heard myself. Imagine how you would sound if you told someone you'd seen Jesus in your toast and he spoke to you. The look on my husband's face was the one you give a small child who says something you find amusingly outrageous. You don't really respond to this sort of thing, you just listen, smile and maybe pat the little person's head. That was the look I got from my husband when I tried to tell him that not once, but twice, I have experienced this incredible moment and heard incredible music.

After that, I decided to keep it to myself. I do Feng Shui for a living, in the South, where I live. That is enough for most people to look at me sideways. Go around telling people I hear cosmic symphonies while I sleep and I might be burned at the stake. I like to be taken more seriously than that. I am not a "woo woo" type of person. My motto in my work is "dismiss dogma, seek results." The things I recommend have concrete, tangible benefits that have been continually verified in my private practice. I say this because I still struggle with fully wrapping my mind around what I experienced. It does not default to the ethereal or unseen, it wants facts and reason and logic.

Come to find out, I am not the only one who has experienced hearing this incredible music. It is something I share with those who have woken from comas or had near-death experiences (NDEs).

In addition to seeing a bright light, it appears that nearing death you also hear sounds similar to Classical music. One man, Stephen Roach of Tucson, Arizona, reported that after a bike crash, he heard "the most intensely beautiful music you could ever imagine" and afterward decided to dedicate his life to "re-creating the exact same sound." The result is "Structures from Silence," a record that, once released, made him realize he, too, had friends. Many people contacted him after hearing his recordings to "tell me that they've heard the exact same music during their NDEs." I found and downloaded "Structures from Silence" on iTunes and, while calming and nice to listen to, it is not what I heard. His creation is soothing, synthesized, watery orchestral bits like what you zone out to during a massage.

Another artist, Melbourne-based Saskia

Moore, after learning that NDEs heard incredible music, collaborated with an orchestral ensemble called *Apartment House* to create *Dead Symphony* a "musical performance and immersive light show inspired by the stories of near-death encounters." It was the feeling as much as the music, of being in the music, or, how Moore describes it, "music heard during NDEs feels as if you are in an incredible wall of sound, surrounding and immersing you completely. Some people spoke of music and light being entwined and together in equal breaths, inseparable if you will. It was this immersive quality I wanted to present."

Searching for alternate explanations let's say that the music I heard was a creation of my own mind. That, while my thinking mind is shut down, unencumbered by daily tasks and visual stimuli, half-asleep and wild, my own little white matter is adept at incredible symphonic creations. I do believe our brains are capable of seemingly miraculous things but that would be truly astonishing.

Like most of us with ears and access to a radio, I have had the benefit of being exposed to a great range of music in my life. I took piano lessons as a child. My mother was a classically trained opera singer who sang in the house, doing her scales and warm-ups before lessons. She made us familiar with the greats and the not-so-greats of the opera world. While growing up, we rarely watched TV. We valued music more.

Later on, in my college days, I sought out different varieties of sound. My musical tastes varied wildly from Bollywood to Indie pop to Hip-hop and Jazz to French Seventies pop and even more obscure genres. So, while my ears have soaked up a scope and scale of music that is likely more abundant than most, I am utterly incompetent and fully incapable of composing anything, let alone a lush, layered symphonic masterpiece no one on earth had ever created even something close to.

Alternatively, could I have momentarily tapped into the communal consciousness of the human race, able to pluck out a symphony the way the idea of gravity fell on Newton or how Einstein plucked the theory of relativity seemingly from the ether? What I am asking is this: do such cosmically towering geniuses own this knowledge or are we all equally capable of tapping into this incredible talent and knowledge during sleep and deep thought the way Buddha gained enlightenment during meditation? If sleep is but a small death, it seems to grant temporary access to this communal genius, musical masterpiece creator-brain.

Perhaps our brains make music all the time, as effortlessly and naturally as breathing, just waiting for us to get off our derrieres and learn an instrument so it can come out. Most days I cram my mind so full with deadlines and to-dos that I can barely hear myself think, let alone hum to my inner tune. Dr. Stephen Halpern, a noted musician and music psychologist, believes that the entire human body is a constant receiver of sound vibration. So while we are walking around or sitting at our desks, not only our ears but also our chakras, the energetic centers of the body, are picking up and processing all the various sound vibrations around us. These chakras are specialized, too. For example, sex chakras, the lowest chakra of your body, are most sensitive to low frequencies, such as bass lines. For sure, we don't turn up Mozart to "get it on," we put on Barry White. Deep, slow and soulful, it stimulates us "down there" because that is the frequency that the sex chakras resonate with. Like a tuning fork, our chakras perk up to their resonate frequencies.

Unless we plug our ears, close our eyes and refuse to touch anything, we are receiving sensory data all day long, whether we are consciously aware of it or not. Perhaps while we are sleeping (or dying), our brain pick through it and put it back together to work things out for the greater evolutionary good or maybe there is no good reason or rhyme at all. Maybe our brain creates this amazing music for shits and giggles to keep it occupied while we autopilot through carpool and the grocery store.

Maybe we don't have to be asleep at all to have an uncommon, ultra-sensory experience. There are some people, namely musicians and artists, that see color when they hear sound. Known as synesthesia, Leonard Bernstein, Tori Amos, Mary J. Blige and Pharrell Williams are among the many musicians that claim this gift. In the autobiography of Tori Amos, entitled Piece by Piece, she describes "seeing" sound in this way: "the song appears as light filament once I've cracked it. As long as I've been doing this, which is more than thirty-five years, I've never seen a duplicate song structure. I've never seen the same light creature in my life. Obviously similar chord progressions follow similar light patterns, but try to imagine the best kaleidoscope ever."

Another musical prodigy, American pianist and classical composer, Amy Beach (1867-1944), had both perfect pitch and a specific set of colors for musical keys. A quote from Walter Jenkins, her lifelong biographer, provides a glimpse into her synesthetic abilities; *"Amy had a wide range of colors, which she associated with certain major keys. C was white; F-sharp, black; E, yellow; G, red; A, green; A-flat, blue; D-flat, violet or purple; and E-flat, pink."* Until the end of her life, she associated these colors with those keys.

Duke Ellington (1899-1974) is another famous musician documented to experience synesthesia. Quoted by Don George in his biography, Ellington said, *"I hear a note by one of the fellows in the band and it's one color. I hear the same note played by someone else and it's a different color. When I hear sustained musical tones, I see just about the same colors that you do, but I see them in textures. If Harry Carney is playing, D is dark blue burlap. If Johnny Hodges is playing, G becomes light blue satin."*

The more intense the note, the more intense the color visualized. For example, red, which has the shortest wavelength and is the most energetically intense frequency, is the color that relates to the strongest rhythmic patterns, followed by orange, yellow, then the calmer greens and cooling off into the lower frequency colors of blue, blue-violet and indigo. Billy Joel's experience is this as well. In an interview with Maureen Seaberg he said, *"when I think of different types of melodies, which are slower or softer, I think in terms of blues or greens...When I [see] a particularly vivid color, it's usually a strong melodic, strong rhythmic pattern that emerges at the same time. When I think of these songs, I think of vivid reds, oranges and golds."*

New research from UC Berkeley reveals we may all be hardwired to associate anything from Bach to the Beach Boys with a certain hue from the color spectrum. According to a study headed by scientist Stephen Palmer, whether it's classical or electronic, we automatically make color connections based on how the music makes us *feel*. This was found to be true for study participants regardless of cultural reference or background. They all tended to link the same compositions to the same color suggesting that humans might share a "common emotional palette" that mixes sound and color interchangeably.

Like athletes' extraordinary muscle memory or a chess champion's ability to foresee nearly infinite possibilities of plays, do we activate some latent super sense simply through abundant use? Or am I trying to explain something truly magical that happened to me, that I was very lucky to experience - a glimpse of heaven with all the beauty and none of the trauma of nearly dying. I guess I won't really know until I get to go back.

Striving to Live Harmoniously

By Janet Mitsui Brown

As a feng shui practitioner, I try to be in balance, harmonious with celestial and earth, and body, mind and spirit. But even for a studied feng shui specialist, it's not an easy task. Every day I hope I feel well, but each day turns out to be different.

Eleven years ago, my husband and I expanded and remodeled our house in Los Angeles with feng shui principles. Upon completion, our property housed our teenage daughter, my 80-year-old mother, my husband and me; all very different people. We each needed a place for study, contemplation and privacy.

We continued to live together in this house through life's transitions. My daughter graduated high school and went off to college, and my mother aged with dementia, then Alzheimer's, and so we redefined harmony almost every day. Today my husband and I still live in the house, but my mother with Alzheimer's moved to a Board and Care, and my daughter has returned after eight years of living away. Talk about transitions, subtle and real, and yet today, we still strive to live harmoniously.

So, let's talk harmony. Simply, I define harmony as being at peace in body and mind. My husband finds part of his harmony in a back house he has named "man's world." I find mine in my work, office and home. When different elements are brought together, and there is an attractive effect that is created, a positive feeling and emotional balance ensues. My belief is that you know when you are in harmony and you know when you are not. It's how to change the imbalance that is the challenge.

So let's begin here. Let's find out if you're in harmony right now.

Examining harmony of the body

Read these instructions all the way through first and then do the exercise, only quickly referring to the book if needed. Put down this book. Close your eyes. Sit with your back straight. You will just sit. Listen to the sounds surrounding you. If they are discordant, then move to a more comfortable, peaceful space. Breathe in and out slowly for five minutes. Ask yourself. "How do I feel?" The goal is to feel peaceful, to feel relaxed, and to enjoy breathing in and out in a peaceful manner, enjoying the foundation of life. But if you don't feel this way, make a note and examine why not.

Now, try to keep your mind quiet while you're doing your daily tasks. It might be quite different!

First, inquire how your body feels. Sit

and feel it. Listen to your breathing and to your heart beating. Are there any particular aches or does some part of your body hurt? Take a moment and sense how your body feels, starting from your head, your forehead, eyes, the space between your eyes, your nose, your neck, and your shoulders. Feel your heart beating, your navel, your hips, and down your legs to your feet.

And gently stand straight (I have to work on this myself). Pretend there is a string lifting your head towards the sky, and remind yourself to do this often, when you're sitting, standing or walking. Do you detect a pain, a blockage, a throbbing sensation? Pay attention to it.

How is your energy level? Are you tired? Sleepy? Do you need nourishment? Answer your body's call (this is something I need to work on also). If you're tired, take a nap. If you're hungry, have a snack. Your body is your baby, your foundation asking for help, and you should respond.

The other day, the Temple I belong to had a summer festival. I had been working in a booth selling Japanese antiques all day, and my feet hurt. I began to notice an imbalance – I wasn't standing balanced on my two feet – instead I was listing on one foot, resting the other. I recognized that I was out of balance and I immediately sat down, focusing on getting some rest, even in 30-second intervals. The point was to be able to stand balanced on both legs, to pay attention to it if it couldn't happen, and to make the adjustment.

Here in the western world, we have a plethora of caffeine offerings, which is a typical lift for fatigue. Most of us use it at one time or another, but, in the long run, an organic solution like authentic sleep or sitting, reading a book, taking a walk, sitting with eyes closed for 30 seconds, is best.

In the end, what is most important is the examination of harmony in your body. If it's not harmonious, find out why not, and work to change it. It's personal and only you can be the judge.

Examining harmony in the environment

I study feng shui extensively, and I believe that using feng shui principles in your environment supports harmony in your life. Take a look around you, and ask yourself if your environment is balanced. Take a look at your immediate environment right at this moment. Is the temperature right and is the light balanced? How is the sound? Right now as I write this, I can hear a constant humming of a machine that is irritating to me. I can choose to close the windows behind me, but the room becomes too stuffy. So, to balance my environment, I have to make choices. And a balanced environment helps me to write this chapter.

Right now, are you motivated to be productive? If not, look around and figure out what is the block, and then work to remove it. When a block is overwhelming and you have problems identifying it, then it is time to call in a feng shui consultant to help you remove it.

If you walked outside, you would probably make natural adjustments in response to the weather. If cold, you would get warm with an appropriate covering. If warm, you would peel off a layer of clothing.

A balanced environment encourages you to be productive and peaceful, and helps you to enjoy life to its fullest. See if you can maintain this attitude in work, travel, and in interaction with family, friends and colleagues.

If you are standing on two feet, balanced, with head straight, and feeling fully focused when life throws you its curves, and there will be many, you will be able to recover. When you are unbalanced, you may fall and then a "domino effect" might occur. Sometimes then, you end up getting hurt, physically or emotionally.

So what is the secret to maintaining harmony?

My dear friend, Olga, is a teacher at a lower elementary school my daughter attended. Olga is a musical maestro, putting together songs, routines and musicals for students of all ages. Every performance I've seen has been unique, lovely to view and hear. Each year there are students with different experiences and performance levels, and yet the productions are always harmonious. How does this happen?

1. It helps to have discipline and routine to reinforce the practice of identifying and maintaining harmony so that it is an organic habit. Every morning I awake and then I proceed to wake up the house: opening shades, windows, letting in light from the new day. I drink a cup of water, and then meditate to start the day, giving thanks for waking up! Then I nourish my body, and my outside garden in silence. This all takes about an hour, but it's a discipline and routine that keeps me harmonious as I tend to my tasks as the day unfolds.

2. Harmony requires patience. Have you ever been a bit late to an appointment, and you are the driver, and you are in the s l o w e s t lane, and there is construction and a lane is closed, and traffic takes forever? Yes, it is so irritating! But to stay in harmony, you have to be patient and go with the flow – be late and accept responsibility for not leaving earlier. Again, harmony requires patience.

3. Find the common denominator of elements. In order for persons to live together in harmony, there has to be a common denominator. Whether you are living together because you are family, for financial reasons, because you like each other, discover the reason and accept it. If not, there will not be harmony.

4. Recognize how unique each aspect

of life is. To live in harmony, you have to appreciate the elements. If you live with others, it helps to appreciate who they are and what they represent. If feng shui elements are to be respected and put together in harmony, you have to know what they are – earth, metal, water, wood and fire, how they are represented, and whether or not they are in a positive cycle. This is why knowing and understanding feng shui principles is so important.

5. When my friend, Olga, prepares her musical presentations, she observes what part each student might excel in. Olga says that after all these years she can tell, intuitively, what makes a student's heart sing. Listen to your heart, and make harmony intuitive.

6. Take a moment and simply enjoy being healthy and alive, for there will be challenges along your path. This is why living with harmony is so important. It keeps you alive, and it enables you to enjoy life to its fullest. If you are not feeling this way, then investigate the blockages and make changes or cures. It's a short life and if you can appreciate each moment, it will bring you joy, and it will bring joy to those surrounding you, both plant and animal.

At the end of the day, I listen to my favorite tune. Currently, it's "Stranger on the Shore" by Lew Ackerman. You should listen to whatever makes you smile, perhaps the soft whistle of a bird or the beauty of silence. Be joyful. You will remember this moment and you will hear all the right notes.

All by striving to live in harmony.

Awaken your Harmonious Side

By Belinda Mendoza

Wherever I go meeting the public…
spreading a message of human values,
spreading a message of harmony,
is the most important thing.

—Dalai Lama

There are many uses for my favorite word, harmony. For this chapter, I chose to focus on harmonious relations.

When one grows up in a dysfunctional family, harmony is lacking. As a child, I became an introvert to shield myself from the chaos around me: arguing parents, heated emotions, drama, and anger. Don't get me wrong; there were good times, but as a child you seem to remember the bad. I sought harmony through perfectionism and pleasing others.

My mom had Obsessive Compulsive Disorder that was undiagnosed at the time. She had to clean the house all of the time, and when things were out of order, all hell broke loose. I have two younger brothers, and I remember coming home from school and making sure that their rooms were neat, their beds were made, and everything was in order so my mom would not be upset when she came home. Even that did not work, as things were still not as neat as she would have had them be.

As I grew up, I too became a neat freak. I needed to have everything in its place in an effort to reduce stress and feel in control. I held sales and management jobs that required discipline and order. While working in pharmaceutical sales, all of my materials had to be easy to get to and packed into the trunk of my car a certain way. If my manager looked into my trunk and it was a mess, I was reprimanded. Through my job, I was repeating my relationship with my mother: I needed to please a person of authority in order to feel okay with myself.

Through my spiritual and metaphysical education, I have learned that you are drawn to what you need to heal within yourself and that my need for organization came from fear. As a feng shui practitioner, my desire for order has become more of a reward than a need to keep peace. I thought that I needed things to be in order to have control over my life, but I have since learned that being in harmony with myself and with the world is an inside job. Harmony should create a sense of peace and wellbeing, not stress.

It took me years to learn this lesson. I had achieved what I thought were the most important accomplishments: I worked for a highly successful medical corporation, I was the only female on an all-male sales leadership team, and I was responsible for millions of dollars in sales; my team and I got along great, I had superb standing in the company, and I was making a six-figure salary with perks and benefits. How could I have all of this and lack harmony?

It is easy to lack harmony without realizing it. I traveled extensively for work, and I had no personal life. When I started to have major health issues, I asked the universe for help. It came in the form of a message after watching an Oprah Winfrey show: Go for the dream, not for the money.

I believed that money would give me the comforts that I did not have as a child, that it would allow me to live well and be happy. This turned out to not be the case at all. I remember speaking to a therapist when I first considered leaving my corporate job. I was so burnt out from trying to do everything right, according to other people's standards. My stress level was at an all-time high. I remember telling my therapist that there was no amount of money that could keep me working for that company and at that pace.

I took a leap of faith and resigned. Coming from a lower-middle class family and being among the first generation in my family to get a college degree, it was a hard choice, but I knew that in order to live a more harmonious life, I needed to make a change. Whether feng shui found me or I found it, it encouraged me to start my own business. I knew how to teach salespeople to be successful, and I knew how to grow businesses. I thought, why not try it on my own? If I did not make it as entrepreneur I could always go back to what I was doing before.

I used my vacation time from work to train in the United States and in China to practice feng shui. On weekends, I helped friends with their homes and businesses; they had success right away, and I developed a following. This was 17 years ago, and I have not looked back. It is the most empowering decision I have ever made. It has not always been a smooth road, but every day I work to live a harmonious life, and today I am a happier and more peaceful person.

As the saying goes, life is a journey not a destination. It is a daily practice. It doesn't just come, you must ask for it, and you must take steps to make it happen. No matter where you are in life, you can make a change to better yourself.

Some things I have learned about living a harmonious life:

1. *Be true to yourself.* For a long time I thought I should stay in my corporate job for the security. Do not deny what you feel. It is your spirit nudging you to move on to get ready for something better coming.

2. *Do what you love.* Yes, we have daily obligations, but every day we make choices that can take us in one direction or another. Choose the one that makes you feel best. When I am not sure, I ask myself: "Is this good for Belinda?" It is not about being selfish and not thinking of others; it is empowering yourself, so you can live your happiest life and help others without depleting your energy.

3. *Talk to people who are living the life you want to live.* They were once where you are. Their secrets can inspire you and reinstate your confidence.

4. *Do not worry so much.* The past is gone, and the present is not here yet. What is in front of you is all you have to work with. I have worry dolls that I bought on a trip to Peru.

They sit on a shelf in my office,
and I give them my worries for the
day. You can use anything from
a spiritual icon like an angel or a
Buddha to a favorite stuffed animal.

5. *Give gratitude.* For 27 days, write
down three things that you are
grateful for on pieces of colored
paper and put them in a glass
jar. This causes you to focus on
what is good in your life instead
of the challenges. At the end of
the 27 days, you will have made a
significant positive shift.

6. *Write down your intentions.* Write down
what you really—REALLY—want
in life. Put these statements in the
present tense, e.g. I am happy, I
have a harmonious relationship with
my partner. Place these statements
throughout the house as reminders.

There is strong energy in thoughts.

7. *Check yourself.* Once a day, look in the mirror and ask yourself how you feel. Whatever is off, fix it right then. Some days I wake up to go to a meeting and I am feeling tired or down, and I put on a bright red shirt to change my outlook. So many times we just do our routine, go out the door and expect the day to go well. It takes a cooperative effort between you and the universe for great results.

8. *Always go for the happy feeling.* Whenever you are not feeling well— whether you are agitated, frustrated, or angered—shift to a happier feeling. Don't stay stuck. Spiritual authors Abraham and Esther Hicks talk about this in their books on the laws of attraction. Whatever it takes to get there, do it. Take a walk,

listen to music, watch a comedy, or hug your child or your pet.

9. *Do not forget to breathe.* This is one of the simplest and least expensive things that we can do to restore our balance, and we take it for granted. Breathing slows our heart rate when we are agitated or afraid, and it nourishes our cells. This can be the first step toward achieving harmony. Take a deep breath, hold it, and as you let it out imagine that you are releasing all of your tension, fears, and doubts to the universe for cleansing and transformation.

Hope you find my tips useful and nurturing. I wish you a most harmonious life with an open heart.

"Happiness is when what you think, what you say, and what you do are in harmony."

—Mahatma Ghandi

The Wisdom Buffet Writers Biographies

Previous Books by Authors:

Journey to Health
Living Well from the Inside Out

Happiness Chronicles -
Short Stories and Recipes for a Happy Life

Janet Mitsui Brown

Janet is a life-long artist. She is an author/ illustrator of a children's book entitled *Thanksgiving at Obaachan's*, a columnist in two Southern California online news journals, Culver City Crossroads & California Crusader News, and a published writer in the Los Angeles Times, the Los Angeles based Rafu Shimpo newspaper, and other journals.

Janet is also the co-owner of *Tani B Productions, Inc.*, a film/publishing production company, and its subsidiary The Joy of Feng Shui, where she is the principal practitioner, advising individuals and businesses on how to enhance their lives utilizing Feng Shui principles.

Janet is a tai chi international gold medalist, and continues to study with the Wushu Center in Los Angeles and Hanzhou, China. Janet formally studies Feng Shui with Helen

& James Jay at Feng Shui Designs, Master Larry Sang of the American Feng Shui Institute, and His Holiness Grandmaster Lin Yun and Her Holiness Khadro Crystal Chu Rinpoche and their disciples, with the Yun Lin Temple.

Based on her experiences, Janet offers consultations in tai chi gong, feng shui, and meditation. Her writings on these subjects can be viewed on her website, and in her ongoing news columns. Janet works with her husband, actor Roger A. Brown, and her daughter Tani, a writer, formerly with Google, and presently a Fulbright Scholar in Southeast Asia.

Katherine Graham

Katherine Graham is a Lifestyle Enhancer and Modern Feng Shui Practitioner based in Atlanta, Georgia. Katherine is known for her powerful, practical and personalized approach to Classical Feng Shui. She is currently writing her first book on Feng Shui, due out in 2015. Connect with Katherine on Facebook and Twitter under Haven Feng Shui, which is also the name of her private Feng Shui consulting company. And, if you're interested in reading about Classical Feng Shui with a Western twist, check out her blog titled, *Feng Shui for the Type A* where Katherine shares her Feng Shui tips and expounds on her motto: "Dismiss Dogma, Seek Results."

Mary Jane Kasliner

Mary Jane Kasliner graduated from Skidmore College with a degree in Health Science and Union College with a degree in Applied Sciences. After nearly 20 years of being a healthcare practitioner, Mary Jane made a radical shift into the world of Metaphysics.

She studied Western Feng Shui at the De Amicis School in Philadelphia and Classical Feng Shui at the New York School of Feng Shui and Feng Shui Institute of London. In 2008 Mary Jane finished her 200-hour national teacher training program in Hatha Yoga at the Center of Health and Healing and Personal Revolution Baron Baptiste program at Yoga Bliss. Several years afterward, she completed her Mastery of Meditation teacher training program under Master Anmol Mehta. Mary Jane also completed Chakra Therapy certification from Bodhi Yoga Center in Utah and additional training in New York, New Jersey, and India.

In 2009, MJ was honored to be a part of Sean Corn's Off the Mat and Into the World humanitarian effort to Uganda where she raised thousands of dollars for orphaned children due to war and AIDS.

Mary Jane has received worldwide media coverage from the Associated Press for her work. She has been interviewed on TV and radio and author of nine books, two online training programs, a DIY Power of Attraction publication, and a lifestyle coach in her *Codes of Creation Mastermind System.*

Mary Jane loves to play golf and travel in her spare time. She can be contacted at www.mjkasliner.com

Kim Klein

Kim's background is in the healing arts, with areas of study ranging from Massage Therapy to Chinese Medicine. Later, as a student of the Rhodec International School of Interior Design, she became acutely aware of the difference in an environment that looks good ascetically as opposed to an environment that actually nourishes our well-being. She started reading every book she could find on the subject of Feng Shui and then attended and graduated from the three year BTB (Black Tantric Buddhist) Masters Training Program, studying the teachings of Professor Lin Yun under teachers Steven Post, Barry Gordon and Edgar Sung. She has also attended many advanced Feng Shui workshops by various teachers, including Seann Xenja, Richard Feather Anderson, Roger Green and others.

Kim is an award-winning author and has written ongoing Feng Shui columns for several newspapers, including the Napa Valley Register and the Santa Barbara NewsPress. She has authored a variety of very popular blogs, including The Coffee Shop Diary along with co-publishing her first novel and screenplay, Nine Degrees North, in March of 2013. Kim recently finished her second screenplay, Twenty-One Sunsets. Her passion for writing is complemented by her experience in a variety of fields, such as Feng Shui, Chinese medicine, multi-media art and design. She is currently working on a novel, Letters From York and has a book in the works about Feng Shui combined with other modalities, entitled Life by Design - creating and living the life you desire.

Located in Santa Barbara, California, Kim currently practices as a Certified

Feng Shui Consultant, working with both residential and corporate environments. She is also a Certified Health Coach and has clients ranging from the Napa Valley to Miami.

(Kim Klein, www.kimkleinfengshui.com, or on Facebook at, Kim Klein Fusion Feng Shui.)

Belinda Mendoza

Belinda Mendoza is a Certified Feng Shui consultant trained in the US and China in East and West Schools of Feng Shui with Professor Lin Yin and Raymond Lo. She is also a Reiki Master and applies energy work to all her consultations. She is the author of *"Feng Shui for the Loss of a Pet, Restoring Balance during Grief and Loss"*, available on Amazon.

She is a former social worker and corporate sales leader. She left those professions and began her feng shui business full-time in 2000. She is a problem solver and has been helping businesses and homeowners create more prosperity through feng shui analysis, redesigns, staging and space clearing for over 17 yrs. Her passions are her yorkies and her work as a mentor in the Big brother Big sister program. She can be reached at: www.designforenergy.com or Belinda@designforenergy.com.

Belinda resides in Austin, Texas and always offers a free 30 minute phone consultation for anyone interested in her services. 512-740-1251.

Mia Staysko

Mia is a professional Feng Shui consultant, artist and designer. Through her company, White Lotus Interiors, she helps people to create spaces that support their bodies, and their souls. Mia's goal is to help people to transform their lives and their spaces through conscious design.

Mia is certified in BTB Feng Shui, studying with His Holiness Grandmaster Lin Yun, Katherine Metz, James Jay and David Kennedy. She has additionally studied traditional Chinese methods, Flying Stars Feng Shui, 4 Pillars Astrology, 9 Star Ki and BaZi with Jon Sandifer and Dr. David Lai. Mia has a keen interest in yoga, numerology and all things spirit-lifting.

Mia is the founding Director of the Sacred Lotus School of Feng Shui and an active member of the International Feng Shui Guild.

Mia blogs on design, Feng Shui and other uplifting topics at www.livingfengshui.ca and produces the digital *Living Feng Shui Magazine.*

James (Jim) Thomas, MBA

Jim has become a successful small business entrepreneur who continues to build and grow businesses. His specialty is computer science however, he went back to school to receive a masters degree in business administration, then became a feng shui consultant.

Jim and Katie own fengshuiemporium.com, luckycat.com, and fengshuidirectory.com. Jim also saw a great opportunity with Amazon/ Kindle Publishing and contacted other feng shui authors for help writing this series of books. The collaboration of authors are known as *The Wisdom Buffet Writers.*

Jim enjoys spending time at his home in Missouri, family, friends as well as his customers from around the world. He loves hiking, water sports, traveling, and exercising.

A special thanks goes to his wife, Katie and his kids, the love of his life. Jim's business coach, Shawn Chhabra, who has guided and helped his business knowledge and to his family and friends for their unwavering love and support.